MW01244326

We Said "I Do" But He Didn't

Carolyn J Galler

Carolyn J Galler

ISBN-13:978-1987763997

615-495-9451

DEDICATION

Glory to God for allowing me to write this book; I pray it blesses others.

Dedication with honor goes to my Sister Evelyn McNeill, who truly supported me in many ways and *always* had faith in what I was doing. This woman of God came into my life when I needed her most, after the death of my mother.

This book is dedicated to all people whose marriages ended in divorce, regardless of the reason.

This book is also dedicated to people who have been a victim of domestic violence, no matter which form it took. Abuse is abuse, whether you can see the scars or not.

Finally, to everyone who beats up on themselves, may this book help you move on and use the wisdom gained from these situations and allow the Holy Spirit to direct your path.

CONTENTS

CONTENTS

ACKNOWLEDGEMENT

First, thanks to God for allowing this test to become a testimony. Thanks goes out to my editor Dana Micheli for supporting me through this journey.

Acknowledgement goes to my co-worker Brownie Sandra King, who truly supported me and *always* gave me wonderful words of encouragement. Brownie truly has been in my corner.

Acknowledgement goes to two of my friends that actually walked with me through this journey, Prophetess Cheryl Fuller and Bernita Perry. These two truly listen, prayed, encouraged and cried with me along the journey.

Acknowledgement goes to my cover designer from Fiverr, nirjhar625

CHAPTER 1

A SIMPLE BEGINNING

Everyone, from their earlier days, has the desire to love and be loved. It is part of being human. Then there are those of us who, for whatever reason, crave love from others because we don't love ourselves. We do things that are not in our best interest to "earn" love or what we think is love. Even worse, we miss the warning signs and red flags that are present in every toxic relationship. Falling head over heels in love may leave you blind when your eyes need to be wide open.

In a small town in Tennessee lived a lady named Cathy and her son Richard, who was in high school. This young man was tall, slender and very handsome. Everyone always gave his mom compliments on how kind and nice he was. Cathy, who was in her mid-forties, wasn't a bad-looking woman herself. In fact, she looked years younger.

This lady had never been the type to go to clubs; she didn't smoke or consume alcohol either. What Cathy enjoyed most was participating in the Jail and Prison Ministry, which she had done for many years.

Cathy's life was far from perfect, however. Truth be told, she had been married and divorced several times, mostly to military men. This is not to say anything negative about men in the military; they just so happened to be the type of men she was attracted to.

Despite her marriages (or perhaps because of them) Cathy was happy and comfortable with it just being her and her children. It's hard for some people to believe, but being single brings its own joys and freedoms. Sometimes we're alone for so long we may even start to tell ourselves that we don't need anyone to make us happy. Then something happens to make our attitude shift again, and that was the case with Cathy.

Cathy worked as a Customer Service Rep at a local cable office. She dealt with so many people in a day that sometimes they were just a blur of faces. Then one day, a man approached her counter looking for help. This man was handsome, smelled great and had a kind voice. While Cathy was trying to act like she wasn't checking him out, he asked how her day was going.

"Good," she replied, then got straight to the point. "How may I help you?"

After introducing himself as Lewis, he explained the services he needed for his home; he also mentioned his two children, who often came for a visit. Cathy found the best cable package to fit his needs, then booked an appointment for the serviceman to come to his home.

Their business completed, Cathy thanked him and told him to have a good day. He responded by asking if she was dating anyone.

Though she was flattered, Cathy politely said thank you but, no, she wasn't interested in dating.

Undeterred, Lewis asked for her phone number.

"I can't give you that information," she replied, "but thanks and have a nice day."

Cathy hadn't noticed that her supervisor, Michelle, had been standing in the doorway and heard the conversation. After Lewis left her counter, Michelle immediately walked over with a smile on her face.

"Cathy, why didn't you give that nice-looking man your number?" she asked. "You're always taking care of others, don't you think God wants to bless you with someone?"

"Yes," Cathy replied, "I'm just not ready yet."

When Cathy arrived home that night, Richard met her at the door and greeted her as usual. She prepared their supper and they sat down to eat and discuss their day as they did every night. But as soon as the kitchen was clean Richard went to do his homework, Cathy picked up the phone to call her friend, Anna. She couldn't wait to tell her about the man who had asked for her phone number that day.

As Cathy spoke, Anna could hear the excitement in her voice.

"You're always turning men down," she said, "Maybe it's time for you to start dating again."

Sometimes people just don't understand where you are in your life. They think you need someone to be happy. Anna did understand, though; she knew Cathy had been abused several times and that's why she decided to take a break.

The first time was when she was just a young girl, around seven or so, when her adult female babysitter molested her. She had also been abused during her marriages; one of her husbands regularly put his hands on her when they argued; once he had been about to punch her in the stomach but was stopped when someone walked into the room. Cathy was pregnant at the time. Then there was the sexual abuse, because apparently he didn't think the word *no* applied to married people. When she filed for divorce, he put a gun to her head and pulled the trigger. It was only by the grace of God and a jammed gun that Cathy lived to tell the tale. It was because of these and other abuses that Cathy had waited on marriage for many, many years.

A few days later, Cathy was helping a customer when she looked up and saw Lewis waiting in line. The other reps tried to get him to come to their counter but he said no, he wanted to wait on Cathy. As she assisted one customer after another, Cathy couldn't help feeling a little nervous.

Finally, it was Lewis' turn. He politely asked her how her day was going, then explained that he needed another cable box, as he'd had an extra outlet connected. Cathy gave him the box and informed him that she would have to call him to send a signal to it once he connected to his T.V. She couldn't help but wonder if he had known he was going to need it beforehand. Was this just an excuse to see her again? After thirty minutes she gave him a call to send the signal. The equipment began to work on the T.V.

Sure enough, Lewis asked her for a date and her phone number. This time she said yes, and Lewis asked if that weekend would be okay. Sure, she said casually, but as soon as they hung up she immediately went to tell Michelle. She then called Anna and told her the news. They were so excited that Cathy had finally given in and accepted a date; in fact, they seemed to be more excited than Cathy! In the back of her mind she could not help but wonder what in the world had she done.

After work ended, Cathy decided to go shopping for

something to wear on her date. This lady didn't even wait until the next day! It appears she was more excited than she let on, even to herself; it appears she had been living in denial.

She chose her outfit carefully. She did not want to give Lewis the impression that she was thirsty or desperate (she was neither!), so she tried to not overdress or reveal too much. After all, when you first meet someone, it's important to be on your best behavior by keeping it real.

The day of the date finally arrived. Lewis offered to pick up her, but Cathy refused, instead saying she would meet him at the restaurant. Over dinner they spoke about their children, their interests and their likes and dislikes. Lewis was a perfect gentleman, and to Cathy's delight, he revealed he had been ordained as a Minister years earlier. The wonderful evening came to an end all too soon, and then with a warm embrace and a chaste kiss on the cheek, they said goodnight.

While driving home, Cathy played the date over in her mind. She had learned that Lewis was younger than her, and she began to wonder how her children would feel about that, should they ever get serious with each other.

A few minutes after Cathy walked in the door, Lewis called to check on her. They spent the next several hours on the phone, talking about anything and everything, and when he asked her for a second date, Cathy didn't hesitate. Over the next few months, Lewis and Cathy grew closer. She hadn't thought she would ever have these types of feelings for a man again.

She tried so hard to guard her heart; she tried not to be too happy because she knew where that could lead. Yet, even after all she had been through, she did not believe all men were the same. She decided to put her past in the rearview mirror, where it belonged.

Oftentimes we forget to leave the past behind us. We continue to think about it all the time and let it rule our present. There are several reasons for this, but usually it's because we never forgave the person or ourselves for what happened in the relationship or marriage. No matter how long it may have been since you were hurt, you can't keep holding on to what Johnny or Billy Bob did to you. It is not easy to let go of all hurts and pains but it is necessary for us to move on.

Lewis appeared to be a good person; he knew all the right words to say and he had done all the right things. Cathy had to admit she enjoyed spending time with him, and they had a great time with his children, who really showed they cared for her. It made her feel loved.

CHAPTER 2

Distance Makes the Heart Grow Fonder

A few months into their relationship, Lewis, who was in the National Guard, was given orders to go overseas. Shocked and very sad, Cathy did all she could to help prepare him for his journey. They put some of his things in storage, and he asked if he could leave some other stuff at her house. Cathy immediately agreed.

Lewis also gave her all his account information - checks, debit card and credit cards – so she could take care of his affairs while he was gone. Surprised, Cathy asked him if he was sure. After all, they hadn't known each other that long. Lewis insisted, saying that something told him to do this, and since Cathy knew she wouldn't do anything wrong by him, she agreed. Those actions made her feel like he truly trusted her. However, as she soon found out, women can assume a man's actions mean one thing when they really mean something completely different. Let's see.

It was a lonely time for Cathy. She missed Lewis, as well as her daughter, who had gone to a university in another state. She took heart in the fact that even though they were separated, her relationship with Lewis had continued to grow. He called and emailed Cathy often as possible and would even send roses and teddy bears to her job for no reason at all. And those mood changes he had from time to time? She believed that was because he was at war thousands of miles from home.

During his absence Cathy made sure she paid all his past due bills and kept his other stuff paid on time. Lewis was so happy about all the money she had saved him while he was deployed; he would tell her stories of how other soldier's wives were messing up their finances.

Still, long distance relationships can be a struggle, particularly if someone has trust issues. Sometimes Lewis had a hard time believing she was faithful during his absence. One Saturday, Cathy and her son went shopping in the mall. Boy, was she surprised when Lewis asked her about "the man" she had been with. Apparently, one of his friends had seen her and Richard from afar and reported this back to Lewis. Cathy wasn't too upset when Lewis brought it up; after all, she knew there were no other men in her life. She simply explained to him that his friend had made a mistake. There were other times when Lewis doubted her loyalty, but Cathy continued to assure him that she was not a cheater. She also told him that without trust and communication they may as well end it. Because of her past experiences, she used to think that people who accused others of cheating were likely cheaters themselves. But she was trying to put the past behind her, so in Lewis' case she dismissed the idea.

One of Lewis' teenage children from a previous relationship stayed with Cathy on her spring break. The fact that Lewis trusted Cathy with his daughter made her feel like this man must really love her. Cathy was not messed up about the child's mother; after all, Lewis had to have an amicable relationship in order to raise their child. Sometimes we make assumptions that turn out to be anything but the truth.

Lewis had been gone about nine months or so and he was due for some R&R. Cathy was thrilled when he asked her if she would like to come visit him in Germany. He purchased her a roundtrip ticket in February, close to her birthday. This would be her first trip traveling outside the United States. Her oldest son, Matt, drove to Tennessee to spend time with Richard while she was gone.

As her trip drew closer, Cathy was truly on an high. She was imagining a romantic journey with this wonderful man with whom she had built a long-distance relationship. She even purchased them identical outfits! Nothing, it seemed, could go wrong.

At the same time, she was nervous about seeing him after all this time. Would she find her feelings had changed for him, or his for her? After all, most of their relationship had been long distance, which is very different from face to face.

Finally, the day arrived. Cathy's friends from the cable company had offered to take her to the airport, so they decided to make a day out of it. They got to the city early and had a good meal, then did some shopping. It wasn't until they had dropped her off and said their goodbyes that Cathy was informed her flight was cancelled. The airlines put her up in a hotel close to the airport so she could grab a flight the following day.

Cathy told Lewis of the change and got into bed, but she couldn't fall asleep. The next morning she went to the airport to begin her journey...again. Several hours later, her plane finally touched down in Germany. It had been a long, tiring flight and it was odd to hear German blasting over the speakers. She was definitely not in the U.S. anymore!

While retrieving her bags, she saw this handsome man standing in the distance with roses in his hand. It was *her man!* As they met and embraced each other, Cathy's heart was beating a hundred miles a minute. He gathered her bags and they hailed a cab to their hotel. *Yeah*, she thought, *I'm about to sin again.*

CHAPTER 3

The Trip Brings a Surprise

The hotel was expensive and quite lovely, though it seemed everything was on a smaller scale than in the States. After unpacking, they headed out for a bite to eat and to get in some sightseeing. They were only staying there one night, Lewis told her; the next morning they would catch a train to the hotel were most military men and their families were staying while in Germany. For Cathy, who had never ridden on a train before, it was another exciting adventure. She sat, all wrapped up in Lewis arms, feeling like this was a love story that would last forever.

After a long ride they finally made it to Edelweiss Lodge and Resort. This place was extremely nice, and more of what Cathy was accustomed to when travelling within the U.S.

Lewis had their itinerary all planned out, including a carriage ride to and a tour of Neuschwanstein Castle. He scheduled other events, too, and expensive dinners with live music. It was everything she had dreamed about, and Lewis was everything she didn't even know she wanted. And just when she thought things couldn't get any better, they did.

One day close to the end of her trip, Lewis told her he felt like seeing a movie; in fact, he had already picked the film and knew where it was playing. Cathy thought it was a little odd that he wanted to sit in the front row, but when she said something about it Lewis just smiled. As they sat in the dimly lit theater waiting for the movie to begin, he suddenly got up and in front of everyone, made a short speech then asked Cathy to marry him.

Stunned and thrilled, Cathy accepted the proposal, then watched as he slid the beautiful ring on her finger. So that's why he had to sit on the front row! This man was certainly full of surprises, which in Cathy's mind was a definite plus. *How on earth,* she wondered, *am I supposed to sit through a movie now?* She was bursting with excitement and wanted to tell everyone she knew.

After the film was over they walked the streets and shopped, then eventually talk turned to what their expectations would be as a married couple.

They discussed everything, from not communicating with their exes to financial decisions; for example, if either one wanted to spend over two hundred dollars they would talk about it with the other first. They also agreed that they would speak with each other before accepting any preaching or other engagements. Certainly cheating and lying were unacceptable. They both agreed they would remain in Tennessee after they were married, which was especially important to Cathy because she wanted Richard to be able to complete his schooling there. At Lewis' suggestion, Cathy would quit her job before they got married and work in ministry.

Cathy also told him that if at any time his feelings changed, he could just let her know and she would understand. She wanted him to think long and hard and pray. She was determined that this marriage would be until death do they part.

Now the time had come for them to say goodbye. As they waited for her flight to begin boarding, Lewis and Cathy hugged each other and cried, knowing it would be about seven more months before he came back to the States. Cathy continued to shed tears as she walked away, while Lewis threw kisses and waved.

As sad as she was to leave Lewis, it was good to be home. Besides, she couldn't wait to tell everyone her news, starting with the two friends from work who picked her up at the airport. On the drive Cathy told them all about her trip, then she showed them her ring. They were so excited for her; clearly Lewis was a very attentive, loving man. Clearly he was her destiny.

Next it was time to tell her children. After thanking Matt for looking after Richard and making sure everything had gone okay while she was gone, she told them about her trip. Finally, she held out her hand and told them her surprise. Her sons appeared to be happy for her. By the time dinner was over Cathy was so exhausted she could hardly keep her eyes open. She went to bed that night still smiling about this most unexpected and happy turn her life had taken.

The next day was a lazy one – Matt went home and Richard went off to school, and Cathy took the time alone to rest up from her trip.

Though Cathy was on cloud nine over the proposal, she was determined to stay grounded. When Lewis called to make sure she had gotten home safe, she couldn't help but remind him of their conversation about their marriage expectations. If he decided at any time that he couldn't honor these things, he should let her know and she would send his cards and checks back to him. When they got off the phone, she even emailed him the expectations! She was covering all bases, she thought.

CHAPTER 4

A Gift, Was it from the Heart?

Though they were engaged, Lewis and Cathy were in many ways still getting to know each other. For example, Lewis didn't know that years earlier, Cathy had been told by a Prophet that God wanted to bless her with a car. She was even given instructions to go pick it out immediately. Around seven that evening she drove to a dealership and picked out a Chrysler 300. After choosing the car she wanted, she then spoke to God, asking Him to please give her the car without a car note. Over the next few years she held on to that prophesy, never stepping out of order to try to make it happen for her, but waiting patiently on Him.

Flash forward to the present. Before Lewis returned to the States Cathy rented a nice home with a long front porch and a large yard. One Sunday after church, she drove to the paint store and picked up colors that she liked, along with the color of the bedroom that Lewis had asked her to get. After leaving the store she saw a Chrysler 300, burgundy in color and so very pretty. Cathy sat in her own car and remembered that long-ago prophesy. With tears running down her face, she thought, *I could never get this car.*

All of a sudden she felt the Spirit telling her to write down the information about the car – the dealership, the price, et cetera - and to take pictures of it. She did as she was told, then headed back home. A little while later, Lewis called to check on her and see how the painting was going. She told him about the car she had seen that day. She did not mention the prophecy. As they were about to hang up, Lewis asked her Cathy to send him pictures and information about the car. Cathy did as he asked, thinking he was just being curious. Then, a few days later, he told Cathy to go make an appointment for a test drive. She did, and it was even better than she had imagined! She reported back to Lewis how the car drove and what the mechanic told her.

Very early one morning, Cathy was awakened by the ringing phone. It was Lewis, calling to tell her he wanted to buy the vehicle for her. Stunned, Cathy asked him if he was sure. Yes, he said; in fact, he had already arranged for her to get another Power of Attorney, one that would give her access to a little over $13,500 – the price of the car!

He didn't even want her to put his name on the title (though Cathy argued this point with him). He just kept telling her how she had done right by him with the money and that he truly appreciated her. After all these years, her prophecy had come true, and the fact that her fiancée had been the deliverer – well, that just told Cathy he had to be the right man for her.

As if having a new home and a new car wasn't exciting enough, Cathy still had a wedding to plan! She bought a beautiful dress at David's Bridal and a flower girl dress for her stepdaughter. She made arrangements for the reception and booked the stretch Hummer limo Lewis had requested for the bridal party. Everything fell into place so easily that Cathy was more convinced than ever that this was truly meant to be.

There was other good news as well. Cathy's son Richard been accepted into a highly competitive medical program chose just twenty students out of over two hundred.

Before she knew it, it was time for Lewis to return to the States. Cathy was looking forward to reconnecting and spending time with their children before they became man and wife. Everything was going as planned, or at least it was until Lewis gave her some news she never in a million years saw coming.

A week before the wedding, Lewis announced that he had been given a job opportunity that could earn him a lot of money. There was one very large catch. The job was in Mississippi.

For a moment, Cathy looked at him, too stunned and angry to speak. In all the months they had been planning their lives together, they had agreed they would be staying in Tennessee, in part they could be near Richard when he finished his school. The plan also included Lewis staying in the National Guard, rather than enlisting in the Army. Now he was completely changing things on her.

Though she was very upset, Cathy knew she had to stand firm. She told him she couldn't and wouldn't hold him back from his career path; if he wanted to go to Mississippi that was fine, but she would not marry him. She would give him the ring back and give him the car. This would all be okay, she assured him, as she wanted what's best for him.

Though it might appear as if she was giving up too easily, the truth was she was trying to do right by him. In the past she had given up opportunities in order to please a significant other, and she loved Lewis too much to do this to him. She would rather give him up. Cathy told Lewis to go pray and seek God about his decision.

A few days later Lewis came back and told Cathy he had decided not to accept the position in Mississippi. He wanted to marry her, and if that meant sticking to their original plans, so be it.

Deeply relieved, Cathy took him at his word. A man's word is supposed to be his bond, after all, and if she trusted him enough to marry him, she had to believe him now. After the conversation was over she felt happy again and reassured that he chosen their life together of his own free will.

The night before the wedding, Cathy's friends and some of her relatives threw her a bridal party. Her daughter cooked up a feast and spirits were riding high. Lewis' family members came too, and Cathy was all smiles as she greeted them in the doorway.

Much of his family was kind, but there is always that one. As she welcomed them inside, she felt this person's animosity toward her. Though that was upsetting, she didn't allow it to affect her; she had already heard many things during their courtship, and it was always about the money. Some of Lewis' family thought she was a gold digger. Whatever their feelings, the night was a pleasant one; they laughed and played games, and everyone seemed to be having a good time. By the time they said their goodnights and headed to their hotel, Cathy felt she won even her staunchest critics over.

CHAPTER 5

A Great Deception

Prior to their wedding, Lewis and Cathy, like many engaged couples, went through pre-martial counseling to make sure they were on the same page. During counseling the pastor gave Lewis a "what-if" scenario in which he had a friend that Cathy didn't care for. The pastor was very thorough – he wanted details of how Lewis would handle such a situation. Later, Cathy would wonder if this had been a sign of issues to come.

The day of the wedding arrived, and with it a flurry of activity. Cathy's daughter and stepdaughter were running last-minute errands, and her son went to pick up her mother, as her daddy was deceased and she didn't want her mother to have to come alone.

Finally, everyone arrived at the church. The large bridal party - six bridesmaids and six groomsmen – all looked stunning in their formal clothes. As she was waiting for her cue to come out, Cathy heard the sound a saxophone, playing a very familiar piece of music. Suddenly she remembered a musician that she and Lewis had heard on an out-of-town trip. When Cathy learned that he had brought the man in to play for their wedding, she was incredibly moved. Lewis was really going all out to make the day perfect.

Her eyes filling with happy tears, she watched as her flower girls floated down the aisle, tossing rose pedals this way and that. Then suddenly, the music changed and everyone in the church got to their feet so they could see the bride. She linked arms with Richard and the two slowly made their way down the aisle. Straight ahead of her, Lewis stood looking incredibly handsome in his white tux.

It was a simple ceremony. First, the minister asked Cathy and Lewis to kneel at the prayer bench and pray. After the prayer, they said their own vows. Cathy's tears started again when she heard Lewis recite his. They were so heartfelt and real. The preacher then pronounced them man and wife and they kissed each other.

After taking many wonderful pictures, the wedding party headed for the reception. As soon they slid into the stretch Hummer the drinks began to flow, at least they did for everyone except Cathy, who was not a drinker. But she laughed and celebrated along with the rest of them as the limo glided toward the wedding hall. Oh my goodness, the place was decorated beautifully, and there was enough food for two weddings! The best part, though, was the greetings and well-wishes the guests called out as they walked in.

The reception had all the usual rituals. Lewis and Cathy fed each other wedding cake and danced their first dance together, cheek to cheek. Lewis placed a chair down for Cathy to sit in, then he got down on his knees, lifted her dress up and removed his garter with his teeth. The bride threw her bouquet and they opened their gifts. When the celebration ended, they climbed into their decorated car and headed home to pack for the flight to Vegas, where they were to spend their honeymoon. The family came by and said their last goodbyes, then the newlyweds fell into bed, utterly exhausted.

The next morning was a rush from the minute they

woke, as Lewis told her he had an errand to run before heading to the airport. As Cathy finished getting ready, he put their luggage in the car, then they drove to the Department of Motor Vehicle in another city. Before leaving for overseas, he had given his brother a vehicle. Now the renewal was coming due, and his brother was out of the area and wouldn't be back in time. Lewis was getting an updated sticker for him.

After completing his business, Lewis returned to the car and handed the sticker to Cathy.

"Look," she said, "I'm putting it in the glove box of the vehicle. We can mail when we get back."

By the time they got to the airport they had missed their flight. Cathy was way too happy to let something like this bother her.

"It's okay," she said, "We'll just catch the next one."

While they were sitting there waiting, Lewis asked Cathy for the sticker.

"Don't you remember?" she said, "I put it in the glove box."

All at once Lewis got angry and mumbled something to the effect that he "couldn't wait to get away from everybody."

Cathy drew back as if slapped. She asked him to repeat what he'd said, and he did.

She couldn't believe what she was hearing. They had been married less than twenty-four hours and here he was talking about not being around everybody, including her. He tried to use the stress of the wedding as an excuse, but she knew something else was up.

But this was only the beginning. Shortly after the plane took off, he told her that he had made a decision: when they returned home from their honeymoon she was to take him to the military base in Mississippi. He had already taken that job.

A flood of emotions – anger, hurt and shock – rushed through her. Even worse, she could not yell and scream because they were on a crowded plane. With hot tears running down her face, she asked him why he had lied, especially since it was a lie that affected not only her life, but her son's. He just kept telling her how great the money was, as if this excused what he had done.

The honeymoon was a nightmare for Cathy. How could she celebrate her marriage when it had taken place under false pretenses? Cathy spoke with her mother, who told her to get an annulment, but Cathy wasn't ready to give up on Lewis just yet. She did not want another failed marriage under her belt. She didn't want to admit to herself that it already was a failure. With that one lie, Lewis, this supposed man of God, had shown her who he truly was.

A few days later, they flew home. Only they weren't going home, but straight to the military base in Mississippi. Cathy realized that when he had put their luggage in the trunk the morning they left, he had included his military gear. It was the longest drive of Cathy's life.

CHAPTER 6

How Will It Work?

When they got to Mississippi, Cathy learned she couldn't spend the night as Lewis had to stay on base with the other military men. In truth, she was glad; she just wanted to go home. She spent the drive replaying the day he had promised he was not taking the job. Other things began to add up as well, like how the "request" that she quit her job before they married had really been more of a demand. She had done so because she thought he wanted to take care of her; now she realized he had accepted the position and needed Cathy to be free to drive back and forth or move with him to Mississippi. Dirty, dirty and tricky – this was the kind of man she had married. She had never felt so foolish, or so angry.

She also thought about the new plan Lewis had proposed while they drove to the base: Richard would stay in the house by himself while she moved to Mississippi. They would give him two hundred dollars a month for food and other expenses.

No matter how many times she played this out in her mind, she came to the same conclusion: Lewis' plan was not going to work. This was not what she had signed up for, but she didn't know what to do remedy it. She decided to pray about it and ask God to lead so she would not get consumed in the flesh.

As soon as she walked in the door Richard knew something was wrong, just as children can always tell when something is wrong with their parents, no matter how we try to hide it. Cathy didn't say anything at first; she just hugged him, then they got all her stuff out of the car and into the house. Finally he asked if something was the matter, and where was Lewis? Cathy could not bring herself to tell him that Lewis wanted to leave him home alone; she just explained that he had taken an assignment in Mississippi for a year or so.

And so Cathy found herself with no work and no money of her own; all she had was whatever money Lewis decided to allot her. Never in all her adult life had depended on another person this way. It was like he wanted all power, and he had succeeded in getting it, at least financially. In the end Cathy decided that in addition to working on the outreach ministry as planned she would also look for a paying job.

In the meantime, Lewis thought he had it all worked out. The military had set him and a roommate up in an apartment, but the roommate wanted to bring his own family down and get them a house. Once this happened Lewis wanted Cathy to come stay with him. The apartment was a large two-bedroom, and pretty nice, and besides, travelling back and forth was too hard. They would barely see each other.

Just the idea of going there made Cathy sick, and no amount of prayers changed that. Over the next few months she and Lewis had a several heated discussions. When divorce came up, Cathy said that was cool with her because their marriage had started with a lie anyway. Though he never called her out her name during this time, he spoke to her in a tone that belittled her and cut her to the quick. When he came home to visit he seemed to always be looking for something to complain about, and he inevitably found it. It seemed there was nothing she could do right.

Truth be told, it brought her back to her childhood, when she felt like she could never do enough to please others, including her own mother. Now it appeared she was in the same situation with her husband. But Lewis had never spoken to her this way before they were married, just the opposite. Cathy couldn't figure out what had changed. Eventually, though, it started to make sense; while he was deployed far away he needed her, and she had done everything he wanted her to do. That's why his narcissistic behavior had not come out.

Still, Cathy held her ground. When she told him she was not coming to stay at the apartment, Lewis blew up. It wasn't the first time, and it wouldn't be the last. After listening to him for a while, Cathy ended the call. And, as always, she continued to cry and pray. She had shed far too many tears in their short marriage, though she rarely did so in his presence. She didn't want him to know he was affecting her in this way.

A few months later, her prayers were answered. Apparently other military guys had broken the rules about having their wives or girlfriend staying with them. After that everyone was told that no one could stay for more than two to three days. After getting the news you would have thought Cathy had just won the lottery; Lewis, on the other hand, was hotter than fish in a deep fryer.

Some people believe they can plot and plan and think God is going to be behind it. At least Lewis always did. Cathy knew better. She knew God was on her side because each time Lewis planned something that would negatively affect her or Richard it always failed.

Still, the situation continued to put a real strain on Cathy. She would go pick up Lewis and bring him home to stay for a few days, which got real old because Mississippi was hours away. Though Lewis was never mean to Richard, he would sometimes tell Cathy that her son was a "sissy" because Richard was more interested in his studies than dating a lot of girls or hanging out at clubs. To Cathy, who adored her son and was incredibly proud of him, this was more hurtful than anything Lewis could have said about him.

CHAPTER 7

Does Lewis Know His Wife's Gifts?

One weekend, Cathy headed off to the base to pick up Lewis. By this time Cathy had started to dread these visits. Lewis had become harder and harder to deal with. The conversation would inevitably turn to what Cathy was doing while he was gone, and it often sounded like Lewis' old trust issues were resurfacing. Sometimes it was all Cathy could to keep her composure, and she knew it was only her close relationship with God that allowed her to do so.

After stopping at the house to drop off Lewis' things, he wanted to drive by the movies and see if anything good was playing.

As they were about to leave the house again, Cathy suddenly heard the Holy Spirit tell her to get the check book. *Do what?* she asked herself, and she heard the same thing. This was unusual because she knew they would use their debit card for any purchases. But she didn't question that voice, she just grabbed the check book and slipped it into her purse.

A little while later, after stopping at the country store, they were slowly circling the theater to see if they saw anything they wanted to watch. Nothing appealed to them, so Cathy pulled onto the street that would take them back to the house. As soon as she did so, she heard the Spirit again:

Pull into that Nissan dealership.

Without hesitation she jerked the car into the turning lane. When Lewis asked her what she was doing, she replied, "The Lord is going to bless you with a vehicle."

Then, as she drove slowly through the car lot, she began asking Lewis, "Do you want that one? Do you want this one?" She got no response. Then she saw this nice blue truck with a hard shell covering on the back.

"There it is," she yelled, "That is the one you're supposed to buy!"

Lewis was looking at her like she was crazy.

"Come on, get out!" She then asked him if he liked it, and his reply was yes.

The next thing that came from his mouth was a confession: a month earlier he had tried to get a four-thousand-dollar loan, apparently for debts he had rung up at the time of their wedding. It hadn't worked out, though, because the bank told him that in order to get the loan he would need a co-signer.

Though she was angry and shocked that he had once again kept a major secret from her, Cathy remained undeterred. When the salesman came out they test drove the vehicle, then she told Lewis to go on in there and get it.

Once again he looked at her like she was crazy. "I couldn't get the other loan for four thousand – how am I supposed to get approved for sixteen thousand?"

Cathy replied, "The Spirit told me to bring you here and you will get that truck, now go on inside."

Without further argument, Lewis followed the salesman inside. After a while he came to the car and told her that he needed to put a thousand dollars down.

"Go back in there," she said, "and tell them five hundred or no deal."

When Lewis came out again he had a look of surprise on his face.

"Baby, you will not believe this! They said okay to the five hundred but the check book is at home."

"No, it's not," Cathy said, explaining that the Spirit had told her to get it when they left the house. She hadn't known why at the time but she knew she had to obey. She then handed him the check book and he purchased his truck.

Really, Lewis shouldn't have been so surprised. While serving his last tour overseas, Cathy, through God, had prophesied to Lewis, even saving him from getting blown up in a truck. Yet he was still shocked that she had known he would get the vehicle that day. It's amazing how some people can be with a person, even date and marry them, and still not know what they really have.

He drove the truck off the lot that day, excited as a baby with a new toy. He was on his best behavior the rest of that weekend, talking about how God used his wife to favor him. For her part, Cathy would continue to make a payment and a half payment each month. After all, she had been blessed too; having the truck meant Lewis could drive himself home for visits, which would save Cathy a lot of long trips to Mississippi. It would also save her from having to deal with him when he was in one of his moods. When he was happy, things were great, like when they were dating. When he was not happy, all he did was put her down, and Cathy didn't want to be stuck in the car with him when that happened. She had already spent too many car rides staring out the window and trying to hold back the tears as he berated her. Most of the time he would bring up something stupid about her past and ask about old boyfriends, working himself up more and more as he went.

There were some good times. On her occasional visits to Mississippi she and Lewis would go to church together. One Sunday, after the singing and offerings were over, the pastor went behind the pulpit to deliver his sermon. Suddenly he paused and said to the congregation, "Hold on a minute… these things are getting on my nerves." He then reached inside his mouth and took out his false teeth! Cathy had never seen anything like it in all her life, nowhere but in that part of Mississippi.

CHAPTER 8

When Will the Confessions Stop?

As time went on, Lewis continued to hide things from Cathy, further eroding her trust in him. It seemed he hadn't heard her when before their marriage Cathy had spoken about how honesty and communication were the foundations of a strong loving relationship; how without them, you're left with little more than sex. Cathy was starting to wish she had taken her mother's advice and annulled the marriage in the beginning.

At the same time, Cathy found herself doing everything she could to please her husband; it was as if on some deep level she believed she had to do everything right so she would not get "in trouble." Cathy was no stranger to this feeling; she had felt it in the past when dealing with an abusive person. In this case, though, it was also confusing, because Lewis had never laid a hand on her in anger. She didn't realize that he was controlling her through emotional abuse, and that words can really hurt you, even if they are not curse words.

He never called her names, but he did belittle her and find fault when nothing was there to find fault with. He still got jealous easily, though she had never given him a reason to doubt her faithfulness; he also seemed to get annoyed when she was invited to preach or speak.

It got to the point when she didn't tell him of these engagements ahead of time; for one, he was in Mississippi and two, she knew he would find fault with something she said. When he was home for the weekend, they attended church together. He would play the happy husband while there, only to pick apart the pastor after the service. If anyone showed any interest in Cathy, he would start an argument, complete with reasons for her to not attend that church anymore.

He also needed people to know she was "his." On one of his visits home Cathy was serving as part of the security team at church. Before taking her position she gave Lewis the tithe check, which was already made out and placed in the envelope. She had no sooner reached the doorway when she saw him beckoning to her. She went to ask what it was he needed, only to find that he needed nothing. He was just making sure everyone knew they were together.

When they got home, Lewis didn't even give her a chance to change her clothes before he started asking all these silly questions, about whether the pastor liked her and if she knew men were checking out her butt when she stood upfront. She tried to convince him that there is nothing going on with anyone but God, but she was becoming very resentful of his interrogations. It was as if he was trying to steal her joy in every aspect of her life, including her most sacred place.

With the exception of their sex life, everything they did resulted in some sort of drama. When he announced one Friday that he was not coming home for the weekend, Cathy was actually happy. Her relief was short-lived, however, for an hour later he called again to tell her he was almost home. She did love this man but his behavior was really starting to drain her. The only way to avoid rancor was to agree with whatever he said, or to talk about his favorite topic: how to make money.

Around this time Cathy began to have female issues, tumors that, though benign, seriously affected her life and might even require surgery.

One day Lewis called and mentioned getting a dog. She immediately told him no. He was not going to be home to take care of it and she had too much to deal with her medical issues and a possible operation to heal from.

He seemed to understand what she was saying, so Cathy was shocked when he came home that weekend with a puppy. It was as if what Cathy said didn't even matter! After bringing the puppy inside with a cage, he took his daughter, who was visiting at the time, with him to Wal-Mart to get some pet supplies. When he returned home, Cathy couldn't believe her eyes – he had gotten a *second* puppy for her to take care of!

He then had the nerve to be angry when Cathy let it be known how upset she was. She was not a cussing woman, but she still got her point across. It was the puppy that took the brunt of his wrath; when, like puppies do, it had an accident on the floor, Lewis began hitting it. Cathy immediately jumped to the dog's side and made him stop, and his daughter became extremely upset and mad at him. Cathy's son came out his room, asking what was going on. It was clear to everyone that Lewis' behavior wasn't about the puppy at all, but about something else altogether. It was like there was a rage inside him. Cathy spent the entire weekend feeling like she had to protect the puppies so her husband wouldn't take his frustrations out on them.

On Sunday afternoon Cathy was lying on the love seat in the sitting room with her feet up; she wasn't feeling well.

She couldn't stop thinking about what Lewis had done the night before, and in her spirit she felt that as he whipped the puppy, he wished he was hitting her. When she heard that she could only say, *Oh no, God.*

A few minutes later, Lewis came in and joined her on the love seat, no matter that it forced her to move her feet.

"You better be glad you're pretty," he said as he looked at her, "or I would mess you up."

There it was, she thought, confirmation that he wanted to put hands on her.

He knew better than to try. Cathy had been in law enforcement; she had also told him about all the abuse she'd gone through in her life. It was a combination he didn't want to mess with. He had no problem with verbal abuse, however, which it just so happened was the only type she didn't know that much about. This is the type of abuse you can't take to the police station; it's the type that doesn't leave physical scars. As far as Cathy was concerned, it would have been better if Lewis hit her, because those pains healed much faster.

Cathy believed that in his mind he was not doing anything wrong. He saw no fault in himself, even when he was lying, which was a lot of the time. Those lies seemed to roll right off his tongue, like when he was talking to females or looking so hard at a woman they saw in the mall that he actually turned around as they passed. When Cathy said something about it he would come up with some excuse, like he was planning on doing a play and she was the right type for it.

But unbeknownst to Lewis, Cathy knew when he was not telling the truth. She had the gifts of discernment and prophesy, which meant the Lord had allowed her to see things that were happening and even *before* they happened. It had been this way since she was a child.

One time she saw a vision of Lewis and some woman in a military uniform having sex. Of course Lewis denied it when she confronted him, but she knew different. Even before they were married, she had shared with him how, in every relationship, God had revealed her cheating husband to her. She thought if Lewis knew this, it would make him think of the Grace of God, and think twice, before stepping out on Cathy.

CHAPTER 9

Time for Another Change

As they approached the year mark of Lewis' position in Mississippi, Cathy prepared herself for his homecoming. She wanted to believe that this might help them grow closer. On the other hand, it could also make things worse, but it was a chance she was willing to take.

One day, Lewis called to – as he claimed - check on things at home and see how she was doing. She told him one of the dogs hadn't been acting right, and when they went to the vet he had to be put down. Apparently, the animal had been ill when Lewis brought him home. When he heard the news, Lewis showed no emotion; he just started grilling her about what she did and didn't she do, as if it was Cathy's fault the dog had gotten sick and died. As sad as she was about the puppy's death, she couldn't help but feel he was better off than having to be around Lewis again.

The conversation briefly moved to day-to-day stuff, then Lewis dropped another bomb on her: he would be home for the weekend, then she would have to take him to Nashville. He had enlisted in the Army and would be stationed in North Carolina.

Cathy couldn't believe what she was hearing; then again, she couldn't believe he still had the ability to surprise her. Right then she wanted more than anything to end it. But how could she? She had no job and was financially dependent upon him. She also wasn't willing to do anything that would jeopardize Richard's well-being.

Before she knew it, it was time for Lewis to leave for his next post. As Cathy drove early one morning to drop him off, Lewis opened the glove box and started rifling through it. From the corner of her eye she saw him pull out a sealed envelope; it was the card she had given him, along with a gift, for their first anniversary!

Cathy tried to control the anger rising within her. "You didn't even think enough of me to even open my card?" She pressed her foot harder on the gas, anything to get this trip over with.

They ended up getting lost in Nashville, and Lewis got angry. Cathy had had enough. Here she was, driving him around at five-thirty in the morning to yet another post he had lied about, and he was angry at her? She slammed on the breaks and told Lewis if he did not leave her alone she would "f**k him up."

"Do it, b***h!" he yelled. It was the first they had ever cursed at each other, and it would be the last.

After that, they calmed down and concentrated on finding the right place. Once they pulled up to the building, Cathy waited for him to find the office he needed to go to, then with a peck on the lips and a curt goodbye, he got his duffle bag out of the car and left. Once again, Cathy found herself making the long, lonely ride home.

Over the next few months the tension between them continued to increase. Cathy visited him a few times, then he took a bus home to collect his vehicle, but other than that they didn't see each other much. She sometimes wondered what he did on his down time. One of his ex-girlfriends lived not too far away from where he was stationed. It would not be hard for her to come to see him, or for him to go to her, especially now that he had his own transportation.

Deep down in her heart she felt like he had reconnected with that old girlfriend. But when she asked Lewis about it, she was met with more denials.

After completing his training, Lewis was able to pick a duty station. He chose a place a couple of hours from their home, a place he knew Cathy did not want to be. It was closer to his kids, though, so she agreed to check the area out. By this time Lewis had gotten really tight with the money. For the first time since being with him, Cathy felt like she had to be humble and submissive, just to get what she needed.

Once again Cathy found herself praying to God to resolve this situation. She really didn't want to go with him! She didn't think she could bear anymore of his behavior, especially in a place she didn't like. He was like a ticking time bomb.

CHAPTER 10

Tell Me How You Really Feel

When he first arrived at his new post, Lewis was staying on base. As always, though, he had a plan. This time it was to buy a condo. Cathy would move in with him once Richard graduated that May.

On one of her visits there, Lewis took her to a place she assumed was the condo.

"No," he laughed when she asked about it, "I rented an apartment."

"But that makes no sense at all," she pointed out, "Why would you spend money on rent when you plan to buy a condo?"

"I just did it," he replied, as if this explained everything.

Cathy looked around and noted that the spare room was set up for an office.

"Okay…" she said, "This is nice, but remember, Richard is graduating in a few months. Where is he going to stay until he goes to college?

Lewis looked at her in surprise. "Maybe," he said, "it could be rearranged for him." Clearly he hadn't given it much thought, if any.

Disgusted, Cathy knew she had to continue protecting her son. She just didn't know how right she was.

Soon after that visit, Lewis decided he could no longer support the home where Cathy and Richard were living. After all, now he had his rent to pay! Less than two months after moving into the apartment, he purchased the condo. The problem was, he had already signed a lease.

Faced with real financial hardship, Cathy again went before the Lord, this time asking for favor with the landlord to allow Lewis out of the lease. When she got her answer, she called Lewis and told him to go to the landlord *that day* and all would work out. He did as she said and sure enough, the landlord let him out of the lease.

While Cathy was relieved, it made little difference in the situation. She was still dealing with Lewis' erratic behavior and the fact that he had control of the purse strings. Through it all, he never seemed to see the negative effect his actions had on her, so Cathy was surprised when he agreed to start counseling with the same pastor who had ordained him and married them.

The counseling really didn't go that well, though, because as usual Lewis did not listen. The pastor even pointed that out during the conversation. To hear Lewis tell it, everything was Cathy's fault. Later that night, as she was sitting on the sofa reading her Bible, Lewis asked a strange question.

"Do you believe I love you?"

"Not really," Cathy replied. She then asked Lewis a question of her own: if she moved to the condo with him, could he promise not to kick her out, leaving her and her son with no place to stay?

In a flash, Lewis got very angry and grabbed the Bible out of her hand.

"I could guarantee you one thing," he said, "and that is tomorrow I could go file for divorce!" It wasn't the first time he had made such a threat. He then added that he could not promise he wouldn't ask her to leave at some point.

It was time to face facts, Cathy thought, there is no way this is going to work. If you can't trust your husband to take care of you and support you without making threats, what's the point of being married?

She had no more time to waste – she had to get a job.

Their next visit was at the condo on Mother's Day weekend. Lewis' children were there too and, always the Betty Homemaker, Cathy was cooking up a storm for every meal.

Right before she put dinner on the table Lewis said he had to go to Wal-Mart and send his friend in another city some money. Cathy felt like that was a lie, but what could she say? He was gone for four hours.

When he returned, Cathy asked what had taken so long, though of course the Lord had already shown her. He lied, then began to fuss and disrespect Cathy, and the next thing she knew, he was telling her to get her stuff and get out.

She didn't have to be told twice. Immediately she packed up all her things and headed for the door. Just as she was walked out Lewis grabbed the door and slammed it behind her. As soon as she left she turned her phone off so she wouldn't have to hear him calling.

As she drove home, Cathy thought about their relationship. Other than sex, they didn't have much of one. When she stopped for gas, she turned her phone back on. Within minutes, it began to ring. She ignored the call, and the several that followed it, until she was almost home.

It was Lewis, telling her she was no longer welcome at the condo. After making it home she called her best friend Anna to tell her all about what was going on and ask for prayers.

CHAPTER 11

Things Go From Bad To Worse

Upset as she was over the state of her marriage, Cathy thanked God she had recently found a job, though she was not making nearly as much as she had been when she met Lewis. She had given up a lucrative position so he could feel like he was the man of the house and that he could handle things. Instead, she had never felt more vulnerable. All she wanted was to be truly loved and accepted, only to find herself married to someone completely incapable of it. Though her world was crumbling around her, Cathy went to work each day and tried hard not to show her son what she was going through.

Shortly after kicking her out of the condo, Lewis tried to cut off financial support. Cathy gathered her information together and threatened to go to the Army with it. He then decided he would give her five hundred dollars a month "until the divorce went through," though at this time he had not yet filed. Cathy figured he had decided it was cheaper to keep her for the time being. She just wasn't sure of the reason.

After months of living in financial and emotional limbo, her sister came to live with her. They would split the cost of the house. For Cathy it was a miracle, and for the first time in months she felt like she could breathe.

A month later, Lewis filed for divorce. By that time Cathy was so strapped for cash she told him that if he gave her twenty-five hundred dollars and agreed to keep her on his health insurance for three months she would sign the papers. Lewis agreed, and they met at the attorney's office. Lewis handed her the money, then they signed the papers ending their marriage. He shook her hand and then left.

Though Cathy knew she was entitled to more money, she didn't push it. She had never been the type of person to try to get over on anyone – even a person like Lewis - and she wasn't about to start now. At times it's better to be free and start over than to hold onto someone and fight.

One week after seeing the attorney, Lewis called Cathy at two a.m. He was crying, telling her that God was whipping him and telling him "no divorce, no divorce." He then he asked her what he should do. Cathy told him to ask God, because she had no answer for him. He must have taken her advice, because the next thing she knew, there, in her mailbox, was paperwork showing he had cancelled the divorce.

Thus began one of the most confusing times in their relationship. After cancelling the divorce Lewis was on his best behavior, and Cathy began to think that maybe she would move to the condo after all. Richard had a job and would be graduating soon, and her sister had moved in so he wouldn't be alone. And, though the struggle was real she and Lewis did have some good times. She decided to try and make it work. This time, Cathy made her own plan. She would get two jobs on base while living with him so she could also pay her share of the house back home. That way if things did not work out with Lewis she would still have a place to lay her head.

It began with a week-long trial period; Cathy took vacation time from work, packed some things and headed to the condo. On the surface, things seemed great. Lewis was so kind to her it almost felt like the beginning of their relationship. Determined to play her part, Cathy decided to do as much she could to make his life stress-free. She kept the house in order and made sure dinner was on the table when he got home from work. Yet she couldn't help but notice that something wasn't right. Lewis seemed to be on his phone a lot, and often went outside to talk. She felt that no matter what he said, her being there was not what he wanted.

While she was there she got some upsetting news. Her sister had to go back to her home to tend to something with her daughter. Without her sister's financial contribution there was no way Cathy could support the house. Not knowing what to do, she turned to God. He had always been with her, and she knew He wouldn't abandon her now.

In the meantime, she had to be practical about her situation, so Cathy did something she never thought she would have to do: she applied for food stamps. Her first and only priority was to make sure she and Richard had food on the table.

Now, during this time she was still having sickness in her body, but Lewis didn't care. The funny thing was he was always telling her that he loved her so much, that, of all his relationships, she was the only woman he'd ever loved like this. Hearing this, Cathy had to laugh to herself. If this was love, she did not want to see hate.

CHAPTER 12

The Class Reunion

During this relatively happy time in their relationship, Lewis came down to attend Cathy's high school reunion. All her children also came to visit, as they too were going to be at the reunion. That night, she couldn't help but be excited to show off her handsome husband to her friends and former classmates.

When they got to the reunion, they found a table of her friends and sat down. Cathy introduced Lewis to everyone, then he told her to go on and visit while he walked around taking pictures. It seemed like things were going great.

Cathy spent some time catching up with Marcus, an old classmate, and Beverly, a close friend of hers. Marcus commented that he had seen her husband taking a lot of pictures, then asked if she thought Lewis would email them to him. He even gave Cathy his business card to give to Lewis just in case he missed him. Cathy said okay, but after he left she immediately tore up the card. She knew if Lewis saw her with Marcus' business card he would immediately think she was up to no good. Instead, she would point Marcus out to Lewis the next time she saw him.

Little did she know Lewis was already watching them. Suddenly, he came up to Marcus and said, "Hey, man, you are not going to disrespect me like that."

Marcus looked at him in surprise. "Like what, man? A few minutes ago I handed your wife a card to give you because I wanted copies of the pictures you're taking." Marcus even added that he was willing to pay Lewis for them.

Cathy was mortified. As soon as they were alone, she pulled the pieces of the torn card from her pocket. But Lewis didn't want to hear her explanations. Instead, he decided to humiliate her further by calling his baby momma from a previous relationship. Oh, he was talking loud and going on just so Cathy knew who he was talking to.

She knew then that the night was over, so she went to find her children. They said their goodbyes as well, then got into their cars and followed Lewis and Cathy back to the house. The whole ride home, Lewis was in an uproar. She tried to explain that Marcus had never been interested in her when they were back in school, and he wasn't interested in her now. Lewis would not even listen.

"I don't give a darn about women," he snapped, "They are all stupid."

Cathy was so furious, it was all she could do to maintain control of the car. How was she ever going to hide her anger from her kids?

Somehow, she managed to play it cool as they walked in the house, but it was only a matter of time before her emotions got the best of her. Everyone decided to play cards, everyone but Cathy, who just sat across the table from Lewis. Suddenly, she noticed the glass of rum her son Matt had in front of him. She had never been a drinker, but when Matt turned his back she picked up the glass and drained it. When Matt poured himself another, Cathy drank that one too.

Now thoroughly intoxicated, she looked at her husband and slowly dragged a finger across her neck as if she was cutting it. She then looked at the big knives on the counter and back at him.

"Mom, are you okay?"

Cathy looked over to see her children eye-balling her.

"Of course," she replied, calm as could be. Thankfully it was late by that time and everyone headed to bed. Cathy lay as close to the edge as possible, so no part of her had to touch Lewis. It is crazy what people will put up with, and for how long.

Cathy had never been a quitter; she always made sure she had done all that needed to be done before saying, "I'm through." Now, she was that point. Lewis' behavior the night before was the worst it had ever been.

The next morning, her children were surprised when Cathy got up to cook breakfast. After the drinks she'd had they thought she'd still be in bed. One thing was for certain, for her to be acting that way, Lewis must have hurt her pretty bad. Always the great pretender, Lewis was behaving like nothing had happened, only this time he wasn't fooling anyone.

After breakfast her children left for their homes, followed shortly by Lewis. When he left, Cathy had never been so glad in her life. They had truly grown apart and she wondered when this was going to end. At this point she was sorry he had cancelled the divorce, for she didn't have the money to get one herself. She would just have to hang on until God presented her with another path.

In her spare time she continued to be a part of Prison Ministry, attending women's conferences and speaking at engagements. She tried to fill her life with many things dealing with spiritual growth. God was her keeper; He kept her from doing something wrong, something not Christ-like.

CHAPTER 13

From One Thing to Another

On his next visit, Cathy overheard Lewis on the phone. He was telling his brother that he'd be coming to see him the following day. She said nothing to him about the conversation, though; she just went about her business. She and a friend had plans to pray together that morning.

The next morning, she heard voices and tiptoed to the front. There she heard Lewis talking about what he was going to be doing to the car once he got it back. With the Spirit whispering in her ear, she went back into the bedroom and quickly got ready, then slipped out to her car.

Once she pulled away from the house she called her friend and told her what the Spirit had said. Lewis was planning on taking the car away, and since he had told her not to put his name on the title, she was going to the license bureau to get the title put in her name only.

On her way, Cathy prayed, "Lord, if this is not what You need to happen, don't allow it. I don't want to do wrong." She then headed with a clear heart to the bureau, where everything went well. Now the title was in her name only. Her business completed, she headed over to her friend's house.

When she got there, she went into full detail of what had happened. Something wasn't right, she said, she just knew it. A few minutes later, Lewis called and asked where she was. He wanted to use the car to pick up his children. "You have the Yukon," she replied, "You can use that to go get the kids."

Immediately, he flew into a rage, demanding that she bring that car back. She refused. He told Cathy that he would give it back to her. She said no. When they finally hung up, Cathy called her son and told him to go find a cell phone and let her know how much it cost, because the Spirit was telling her that at some point Lewis would be cutting her phone off.

Lewis continued to call until she told him to leave her alone, that she didn't know when she'd be back home. In the meantime, Cathy's son came to get the money for the phone. Cathy, being led by the Holy Spirit, then called her older son and daughter and let them know she believed Lewis was going to cut the phone off and she would contact them with a new number soon.

Lewis called Cathy again, this time telling her he was going to report the car stolen and she was going to jail. That's when she let him know that she'd obeyed the Spirit and also that she'd heard his conversation the night before. She knew something was up, she said, when his brother came to their house early that morning.

At this point Lewis was so enraged that Cathy began to fear for her safety. Thank God he didn't know where her friend lived! Before her son could return with the phone, Lewis indeed cut her cell phone off. By that time she had already contacted her friend Shirley in St. Louis and asked if she and Richard could come stay with her for the weekend. Shirley immediately said yes.

Next, Cathy called a neighbor who lived across the

street and asked about the vehicles in the yard. From what the neighbor said, Cathy assumed Lewis had left to go get his children.

With the coast clear, Cathy and Richard went to the house and got clean clothing; and, because Cathy didn't trust Lewis' brother, she also collected any information with her social security number on it. She knew he was going to be looking for the title. The Spirit told her to take all paper from the house and she did.

A few hours later, she and Richard made it safely to Shirley's home. She was so sad and hurt and tired of Lewis; their marriage had felt like one big roller coaster.   At least she took comfort that Richard was glad to see his old friends.

Shirley and Cathy went to the store and then back to her house, where they talked until late into the night. By the next morning Lewis had turned her phone back on. It had simply been a punishment. By that time, Cathy didn't care. She waited until late that evening to head home, that way Lewis would have already gone back to the base to report for work.

Lewis might have been gone, but there was evidence of him all over the house. Things had been moved around and messed up, and he had left notes, handwritten on yellow legal paper, plastered all over the place. He had written how sorry he was, and that he would never try and take her car again. Those sheets of paper confirmed her suspicions. It also proved that once again the Spirit had been protecting and guiding her.

The next time Lewis called, it was with another apology. He then told her that the night he had his children, he became ill and had to lay down. It had gotten to the point he could barely breathe and he couldn't call Cathy because he had cut her cell phone off. He had been in a really bad way and couldn't call an ambulance because he had no one to watch the children.

Cathy had no pity for him, not after all the terrible things he had done to her. Before they hung up she did tell him she hoped he felt better. She couldn't understand why this man kept holding onto the marriage when he so clearly wasn't happy. Why wouldn't he set them both free?

CHAPTER 14

A Crazy Experience

Shortly after this incident, Lewis decided to move more of his things to the condo. His brother had promised to come and help load the truck, but when he did not show and didn't answer his calls, Cathy asked Richard if he minded helping. He agreed, but they had to be done by the evening because he had plans. Lewis promised he would have them back by five o'clock.

They began to load the truck up with furniture and Lewis' other items, then started off on the two-hour drive. They were making pretty good time, and Cathy and her son both assumed they would drop the load off and get right back on the road. But, as usual, Lewis had other plans, like giving them one task after another, even making them look for stuff he could have found later on his own.

After they'd finished putting the last things in the place, Cathy and Richard went and sat in the U-Haul, thinking Lewis would be out in a few minutes. Wrong. Finally, Cathy went in the house and told Lewis to come on because they were not going to make it back in time for Richard to keep his date. She then went back to the truck, upset that he was holding her son up so long. When he eventually did come out he was clearly mad, and even yelled at her in front of Richard, which had never happened before. Cathy was so heated she wanted to throw that wedding ring in the weeds.

Lewis drove too fast on the way home, partly because he was mad and partly because he had given his word to

Richard. After what seemed like forever they arrived home, and Lewis gave Richard cash for his troubles.

Richard ran inside the house and got ready for his date. Cathy and Lewis seemed more apart than ever. Cathy had decided she was not going to sleep in the bed with him that night. When he stepped out for a few minutes, she took a shower, put on a black hoody and black stretch pants and lay down on the chaise to watch television. Suddenly, she heard a voice tell her to keep her purse and car keys close to her. She did not understand what was going on but she obeyed.

It wasn't until the next morning that she realized Lewis had slept on the living sofa. He waited until Richard had left for church, then went looking for Cathy.
God had told him destruction is at hand, he said, and she needed to get herself together.
"Well, I also received a word from the Lord," she replied, "and that was not what He said."
She then let him know that the message was for him; God was not pleased with his behavior the day before, or the way he had treated her in front of Richard.

The next thing she knew Lewis was telling her that he needed to pray with her. He slapped his hand across her forehead and as he was praying Cathy's eyes were open and looking directly into his. What she saw there scared her. Finally he finished praying and went into the bedroom, only to come back a minute later. He grabbed Cathy and took her to the bathroom and asked her to look in the mirror.
"Look at yourself," he said, "What do you see?"
"I see myself," she said, and he replied, "No, I see a devil."

Suddenly she felt the Holy Spirit letting her know that if she didn't escape, one of them was not going to make it out of the house that day.

Lewis then announced she was not going anywhere that day; he was going to keep her held up in the bedroom. Fearing for her life, Cathy grabbed the scissors she kept in her tray in the bathroom. They tussled over them until he eventually got them away from her.

Cathy managed to hit Lewis and he let her go.

"Hit me, devil," he yelled, "Go on and hit me as long as I get my wife back."

Cathy felt like this was her opportunity, so she hit him right in his face. She then pretended she wanted some water, but he told her to drink from the bathroom sink because she was not getting out that room.

The whole time Cathy had been praying she'd get out of this alive. Suddenly she heard a voice say, *Pretend you want to get affectionate.* She started talking sweet, and his demeanor started changing. She told him, "Baby, let me go get some bath towels, so I can get all fixed up for you."
Lewis fell for it. Cathy slipped on her slides and took off, grabbing her purse on the way out. She was shaking as she got behind the wheel and drove to her friend's house; she had never seen Lewis act this crazy before.

On the way she called Richard and told him not to go home; she would let him know when it was okay. Cathy knew Lewis had to report for duty the next morning, so around seven that evening she checked things out at the house and went home. Again, there were "I'm sorry" notes plastered on the wall. This did little to calm Cathy's fears; she knew there was a demonic spirit in him, so she went and purchased a new lock for the back door. It was installed that night.

CHAPTER 15

The Straw That Broke The Camel's Back

A few months later, Lewis delivered another shock: he had signed them up for a marriage retreat offered by the military. Richard had now graduated, and Lewis thought it was a chance for them to start over again, as well as celebrate their anniversary. Cathy just hoped it would be better than the last one.

The year before, she disappeared from the breakfast at the hotel where they were staying. Lewis was still nitpicking at her about the class reunion and just being abusive in general and she couldn't take it anymore. She went outside and began to climb on the metal railing surrounding the body of water; something was telling her to jump in. Suddenly, a spirit of hope came over her and she got down. Lewis didn't bother to come look for her, so after a while she went back inside, all the while praying that this nightmare would one day come to an end.

Now another stressful year had passed, and Cathy found herself once again agreeing to do what Lewis asked. On the weekend of the retreat he picked her up for the hundred-mile drive to the hotel. Imagine Cathy's surprise when he showed up, not in the Yukon, but the brand-new Nissan he had purchased without a word to her. As they hit the road he was all happy and she was thinking, what the heck? But she held her tongue and for once they had a pleasant drive. When they arrived they checked into their room, then went for a meet and greet. Everything was really nice, but Cathy couldn't help but notice how fake Lewis was being. Anyone who saw them would have thought he was so in love. Cathy knew better, though. For a man who said he loved his wife he certainly had a poor way of showing it. It made her feel sick.

The next morning was a couples' breakfast, followed by their first session. Early that morning Lewis claimed he had work to do at the base. He promised to be back in time to eat breakfast with her, and though she knew he was lying about work, Cathy waited until the last thirty minutes to go eat.

Seeing she was sitting there alone, a high-ranking officer came over and asked her where Lewis was. When she told him, he said Lewis didn't have any work to do, as attendees had been given three days off for the retreat. There it was, verification of another lie. She had known from the way he was acting the night before that something wasn't right.

Finally, just as class was about to start, Lewis walked in and kissed her. Another show, as he knew she was boiling that he had missed breakfast. Unaware that the officer had revealed his lie, he continued to talk about "the work" he had to do, but Cathy let it go. She was a true believer that what is done in the dark will eventually come to the light.

The exercises in class made her feel like they were just going through the motions. Whenever there was a break he didn't stay with her, but chose instead to walk around the parking lot while talking on the phone. Cathy did meet a female military personnel member she could vent to; she also asked questions she thought might be helpful to her later on.

By the last day of class, Cathy didn't feel she had learned anything she didn't know before. Neither did Lewis. The whole time he had tried to find something to pick a fight about. He often complained, especially when they played games and lost. As soon as the event ended they packed their car and headed to their home, or at least to Cathy's home. It was the day of their anniversary.

While in the car, Lewis received a phone call and from the way he was talking she could tell it was a female. As usual he said it was business, but she knew better. When he finally hung up, Cathy pointed out that they had just gone to this marriage retreat to help get things back together and he was still being untruthful to her. It was September, and Cathy and Lewis had planned on coming together as a family by the end of the month, or certainly by the second week in October.

The more she thought about it, the more the lies and omissions began to add up. First there was the new Nissan she had known nothing about, then there was the mysterious "work" he had to do. Now there was the strange phone call. As they got closer to Cathy's house he suddenly seemed to be in a rush. He told her he had to go back down the street to get gas. She knew he just wanted to be alone to call the person on the phone back.

Cathy had thought they would do something special for their anniversary before he headed back to the base. She didn't say anything, though, just grabbed her things from the trunk.

A while later she heard a car and looked out the window. Lewis was sitting in the driveway talking on the phone. Knowing it was another woman, Cathy went outside and knocked on the car window. He lowered the window, then sat there looking stupid while Cathy called him out.

He didn't really seem to care until she kicked the front of his new car with her foot. She then went into the house and he immediately got out and checked the car for damage. Finding none, he went inside just long enough to tell Cathy she better be glad she didn't do any damage; then he left and headed for the base.

The next few days was one frustrating conversation after another. Sometimes people don't realize that changes in their behavior, even subtle ones, are an indication of something more serious. A change can sometimes mean a new person is giving them attention, or they may even be having a full-fledged affair.

To Cathy's surprise, Lewis admitted that he didn't understand how she could have been so faithful to him while he was deployed all those months. If the shoe had been on the other foot, he could not have been faithful to her. Finally, he was being honest! Cathy told him if only she had known how dishonest and self-centered he was, she never have dated him, let alone married him.

Every time they hung up the phone, Cathy asked herself why she was still with this man. She told herself that when it was finally over, she wanted to know she had done everything possible to make her marriage work.

CHAPTER 16

What's Done in the Dark Will Come to Light

Though Cathy knew Lewis had continued to lie to her, she was determined to give their marriage another chance. To justify this, she reminded herself about the good times they'd had together. It didn't help matters that Lewis was such a smooth talker.

The first week of October, just as they were about to move in together, Cathy had a vision even she could not believe. The Lord revealed to her that Lewis had gotten someone pregnant. Cathy woke up in a confused state. This lady knew God had dealt with her like this all her life; no matter good or bad, He had warned her of many things that were about to come up on her and others in her life. Still, she continued to sit up in the bed with a look of disbelief until it was time to get ready for work.

When she got there, Bernice, a close friend with whom she shared her marriage issues, came into her office. Cathy told her about the vision and what the Lord had revealed to her. Cathy knew deep down inside she was being prepared for the news. Who knew her any better than God?

Bernice gave her own take on the vision and the word, which was that they were probably accurate. It wasn't easy for Cathy to hear. She spent that whole long day wondering when this would be revealed to her. Cathy wanted it to happen before she made the mistake of moving in with Lewis. In the meantime, the only thing she could do was wait.

Lewis continued his usual behavior. He took her to a military ball, and oh my goodness, he knew his wife looked beautiful. But before the night ended he had something to say because some guy at the table had been talking to her.

The next week she got a call from Lewis. He began by telling Cathy how much he loved her and that he never meant to hurt her. He had always been surprised that Cathy even looked his way. Suspecting something was up, Cathy waited for him to get to the point.

That's when he said it: he believed he had gotten someone pregnant.

"Okay," Cathy replied. She then told her shocked husband that God had already let her know. "Now," she said, "You know what you need to do."
Lewis claimed he did not want to be with that female.
"Well you will be with her for the child's sake," Cathy said, "and if you didn't want to be with her you would not have had sex, or at least you would have worn a condom."

That's when Lewis started telling her his "plans." One was that he and Cathy could raise the child together, and that he could send the mother child support and he and Cathy could continue being married.
"Thank you, but no thank you," she said. She then told Lewis she just wanted him to leave her alone and she would not be moving in with him. He needed to go file the divorce papers because it was over. Somehow she managed to say this without raising her voice, and before they hung up she added, "May God be with you, Lewis."

It was only after they got off the phone that she

allowed her true emotions to come out. She was so hurt that he had gone this far. He should have just allowed the divorce to go through the first time! For the life of her, she still didn't understand why he hadn't, not when he so clearly wanted his freedom to run around.

The next day she called out from work; she just wanted to be alone and figure out what in the world was she going to do next. Cathy knew she couldn't afford to stay in that house much longer, even though she was going to demand that he give her money until the divorce was final. Lewis continued to call, but she ignored him. Anything else, she figured, would have been foolish.

As time went on, Cathy got a supervisory position that paid more money. Lewis continued to visit, always asking if she had someone. Her reply was always the same: no, she didn't. No matter what he had done she was still a married woman.

Though outwardly she kept it together, Cathy was a hot mess, filled with anger and hurt. She couldn't believe she had another failed marriage under her belt. She spoke with Lewis less these days because she didn't want to hear the things he said about the woman carrying his baby. He just didn't realize that she didn't care about the other woman; Cathy didn't have low self-esteem. She had just gotten with a wolf in sheep's clothing.

While reading this story, you may wonder how this can happen, how this strong woman had gotten into in a bad situation and allowed herself to be emotionally and financially drained. Like any abuser, Lewis had gotten her where he wanted her to be, dependent on him. But Lewis didn't realize that the God she served would bring her out of this, as He had always done before.

Cathy could have reported the infidelity to the military authorities; she knew this from speaking to a friend on the inside. But she didn't want to do that. Foolish as that may have been, she was the type of person who truly believed God would take care of him in the end. So she began to focus on what made her happy, and that was ministry and helping others. She got involved with CASA – Court Appointed Support Advocate. They even recorded a video of telling her story of being adopted as a child, which was very exciting for her.

Through it all, Lewis continued to come by, telling her how he loved her and not the other lady, Loretta. He also told Cathy that he was about to go to war again and he may need her help. He was thinking about putting his car in storage and that he may need her to keep an eye on the condo.

The entire time he was talking Cathy knew in her mind that Loretta would be the one taking care of things for him while he was away. She was done managing Lewis' affairs.

Cathy was the type of person who did not like confrontation. So instead of calling him out she just always let him think she believed what he was saying. She did, however, turn down his invitation to attend the ceremony when they shipped out because she knew the other woman might be there.

CHAPTER 17

Time for A Change

A few months later, Cathy moved into a two-bedroom townhouse. She loved having the extra bedroom because she could always open her door up to anyone who needed help, even a person outside her family.

The best part was that she was starting over again in a nice place - without her husband. She tried to push him to get the divorce prior to leaving, but he always made excuses and blamed her when he was the one in control. She didn't want anything but health insurance until she had her surgery and was fully recovered. During this time she still required him to pay the five hundred dollars each month for support.

She knew what she could have done to him. She had spoken to an attorney and when she gave him proof of everything, he wanted her to take Lewis to the cleaners for the pain and suffering he had caused. He especially wanted to hold Lewis responsible for the changes in her lifestyle since he told her to quit her job, which she had in writing.

The problem was she didn't even have the money for the lawyer or the divorce, so she continued to wait on Lewis. With a baby coming she would have thought he'd want to get it over with, but instead he continued to lie, like she was the one holding everything up. He just didn't want to let Cathy go for good.

While deployed he continued to reach out to Cathy with emails and phone calls. One time he texted Cathy to tell her that Loretta was not doing well with the pregnancy. They were even concerned something might be wrong with the baby. This man had the nerve to tell Cathy to pray for them! Just a few weeks earlier he had texted her telling her how his baby was growing so fast. Eventually, she stopped reading his messages altogether.

After years of discomfort, Cathy finally scheduled her surgery. It was a major operation, which was why she was having it while he was gone. She was nervous enough already.

On the day the operation was to be performed, Richard and his future wife were there by her side. They waited until the surgery was over and supported her. While in the hospital she received a phone call from someone telling her that Lewis' baby had been born and was not doing too well. No matter how she felt about Lewis, Cathy began to pray; after all, the child was an innocent.

When she was finally discharged, her oldest son and his wife came down for a few days to assist with her needs. After they left Cathy received a phone call from her friend who worked at the base. She told her a woman had come on post pretending to be Lewis' wife. She needed Lewis to come back because of the child's situation.
Apparently, they had sent a Red Cross message to Lewis, trying to get him back to the States.

All Cathy could think was, when is this nightmare going to end?

To add insult to injury, the next day Cathy received a call from the wife of Lewis' friend who was serving with him. This nice lady was calling because she'd heard Lewis' "wife" had delivered their baby and she wanted to reach out and see how they were doing.

Furious, Cathy informed the lady that Lewis' mistress was the one who'd had the baby. "Yes, I'm still his wife," she said, "and I've just had major surgery, but there is no baby."

After an awkward moment, the woman apologized and got off the phone.

Shortly after he made it to the States, Lewis called Cathy. She told him about the phone calls, not that it made any difference at this point. He told Cathy he was going to do a blood test to make sure the baby was his. "I know the baby is yours," she said, "and I know he is sick. I prayed for him."

Finally, she told Lewis not to worry about her; he should take care of Loretta and the baby because they were his family now.

She then blocked his number so she could focus on her own healing.

It was a long journey because not only was she healing from her surgery but from her broken heart as well. Aside from her friend from the army base who came and brought her some fruit, Cathy kept her distance from people because she didn't want anyone to know what her husband had done.

Many people, especially Christians try and act like everything is fine in their home when it is a hot mess. People can be so dressed up on the outside and be so bruised on the inside. Cathy was no different, and during this time she spent a lot of time asking God to please show her the lesson in all of this.

Marriage is hard enough, even more so when, like their marriage, it is based on many lies. The real truth is that God gave her strength through all of her trials the entire time

CHAPTER 18

The Struggle Is Real

After six weeks of recuperation, Cathy was finally able to go back to work. She was so happy she could truly focus on getting her life back together instead of lying in that bed day after day, week after week. She even began doing overtime to make more money and to occupy more of her time.

Very early one morning, Cathy got up and dressed; they needed extra help at work and had asked her to come in. She was just about to get into her car when they called her and told her not to come. It was still only four-thirty in the morning, so she went back inside and got undressed. She had just slipped into bed when the phone rang. Of all the people she thought it might be, Lewis' baby's mother never entered her mind. As soon as Cathy answered, Loretta started asking her to stop calling his phone. Well, wasn't this something!
"It wasn't me," Cathy replied, "It may be another woman he is seeing."
She also pointed out that if she were the type of woman to cause problems she would have done it long before now. "You know," she said, "He *is* still my husband - no good and distrustful - but my husband all the same."

Immediately, Loretta changed her tone, and the two had a long, calm conversation. It would be the first of many. After their conversation, she would periodically call Cathy, supposedly to chat, but Cathy wasn't stupid. She knew Loretta was just trying to see where Lewis' head was regarding his feelings for Cathy.

The calls even continued after Loretta and Lewis were married! Loretta would call to get Cathy's take on issues they were having. Cathy had the feeling that Lewis was going to treat Loretta even worse than he had treated her. She even told Loretta, "Different actress, same actor. The movie will be a similar plot but the abuse will go to another level."

Sometimes Cathy even felt led to pray with Loretta on the phone. After all, who was in a better position to support her than someone who had dealt with Lewis firsthand? For a long time Cathy was there for her, but eventually, Loretta time was up as well. Like Lewis, Loretta didn't know that Cathy knew when she was lying to her, and Cathy didn't bother to clue her in. She just let her think that she believed everything she said. When you are a true child of God, He will not let you be fooled. He will show you the truth, and it is up to you to decide to believe or deny.

Sure enough, the same "movie" did play out for Loretta and Lewis, to a degree that even Cathy couldn't have anticipated. Apparently, Lewis had gotten yet another woman pregnant! People may ask why Loretta didn't leave him then, just as they wondered why Cathy stayed with him through so many trials and tribulations. There were several possible answers to that question – including the fact that Loretta had a young child to worry about. She also may have craved love so badly she was willing to take whatever Lewis dished out. Whatever the case, she stayed with him even after he got his mistress pregnant for a second time.

At this point Cathy thanked God she'd had her tubes tied all those years ago. Of course she told Lewis about this before they were married, and he'd commented that if they could have children, he would have kept her barefoot and pregnant. It was just one more way Lewis maintained control over the women in his life.

Loretta may have believed in the beginning that Lewis really wanted more children and that's why he stepped out on Cathy. But after he did the same thing to her, she could no longer deny the truth. Stepping out was just what Lewis did, no matter what woman he was with. He never knew the value of what he had at home.

As angry as Cathy had been when she found out about Loretta's pregnancy, she could feel nothing but compassion for what the young woman was going through now. Loretta had fallen prey to the same charm she had, and now she was living with the consequences. And just as Cathy had predicted, the abuse did escalate to physical violence, both toward Loretta and the woman he cheated on her with.

The moral of the story here is that Loretta should have done her homework. If she had, she would have realized that when they first started seeing each, Lewis possibly showed her the *cancelled* divorce decree in an attempt to convince her that he was free and clear.

With the resources we have today, there is no need to accept such a thing at face value: go online, search records and make sure the divorce is final. It may sound cynical, but the truth is there are predators out there who will take advantage of a trusting person. There is nothing wrong with protecting yourself; in fact, it is your God-given right.

This was one of Cathy's lessons. She went through a lot of pain to learn it, but in the end she did so while remaining true to herself. Cathy knew inside that she done all she could do to please and support that man, but she drew the line at forfeiting her life for him. She also could have hurt Lewis as badly as he hurt her, but she refused to throw stone for stone. This lady was a strong believer that one day he would get his. As a child of God, she knew you truly reap what you sow in life, one way or the other.

CHAPTER 19

Some Do's and Some Don'ts

Marriage is the oldest promise and vow made between two people. Indeed, the Word tell us to be equally yoked together. Yet marriage it also perhaps the most challenging relationship we can engage in. We can look in awe and admiration at people who have been married for twenty years, but we don't know what struggles they've endured, or what they continue to face on a day-to-day basis. Everyone deals with these struggles differently – one couple may divorce over an affair, while another uses it to renew their faith and commitment to each other.

Once free of Lewis, Cathy could see all her mistakes and would hope never to make them again. As for Lewis' mistakes, she would have forgiven them if only he had had been willing to work on his issues and truly commit to an honest marriage. She would have even supported the child he fathered outside the marriage.

When doing your "due diligence" before marriage, it's important to realize that premarital counseling only goes so far. Sometimes it's because the couple is so focused on being in love they agree to most of the stuff the preacher talks about; other times, as in the case of Lewis, one person may pay lip service to the preacher with no intention of following through after the *I dos*. They just agree to everything in order to get what they want.

Cathy is not a marriage expert but speaks from her knowledge and experiences. Marriage is not a nine to five job, but a twenty-four-hour, three-hundred-sixty-five-day a year calling. If you are not willing to give one hundred and ten percent, don't bother.

During your years of marriage you must learn to fight fairly, apologize, find a resolution, listen and be able to learn. No person on this earth is always correct, even though there are people who like to think they are. Some will do anything to appear the "winner," including twisting facts and words to suit their needs. They are master manipulators.

Others vow, "'Til death do us part," but what they really mean is "'Til I don't like the circumstances anymore" or "'Til things get too challenging," et cetera. For example, some people cannot handle when their mate gains weight or experiences some other kind of health issue. If you're thinking of getting married, consider such a scenario. Would you cast your mate aside, or would you kindly and considerately motivate them (i.e. sharing a work-out plan and encouraging them to eat differently)? If you chose the first answer, you are not ready to get married!

A true marriage is fat or skinny, hair loss and financial loss, and whatever else life throws your way. So without a shadow of a doubt you need a person who won't abandon you just because the going got tough.

When considering marriage you must look much deeper than the flesh and into their heart. Examine their lifestyle and, if their parents are living, how they treat them. And don't just accept some story about what momma or daddy did to them years ago as an excuse for not communicating with them. Look for the signs of unforgiveness and an unwillingness to compromise, for surely those signs will be there if you only have the courage to open your eyes.

Cathy heard once that everyone should see their mate extremely mad during courtship so they'll know what they really would do or how they would react. Looking back on her relationship with Lewis, she feels she should have taken that advice.

Spending time with your mate is extremely important, not just "hanging out," but real, quality time that allows you to really get to know each other. Do a variety of things together so that you can see different aspects of each other's personalities. This is especially true of people in long distance relationships, where there is a lot of opportunity for people to put their best face forward and pretend. Spending a lot time together will put an end to the show and force the real Mr. or Miss Jones to stand up. This was another thing Cathy feels caused her to be taken in and, eventually, controlled by Lewis.

Cathy also learned a particularly important lesson with regard to people who claim to be Christian or living a Godly life. If, like Lewis for example, they say they are a minister, don't just accept this at face value and get caught up in the flesh. Try the Spirit by the Spirit. Satan can come in the form of the best-looking person and know the Bible front to back. Remember, he has peeped into your future and will do anything and everything to prevent you from claiming God's blessings.

At the same time, listen to what the Spirit is telling you. In the beginning, Cathy's first instinct was to turn Lewis down. Was this the Spirit talking to her? She believes so. It was only when she started listening to people that she stepped away from the Spirit mind and went into the flesh.

Whether we realize or not we have all heard from the Spirit at one point or another. Oftentimes our first instinct is to test the message to see if we are going crazy or making it up. Why don't we practice such discernment with the people in our lives? When you are dating someone, test that person to see if he/she cares about what concerns you. If they do not – end the relationship. For example, if you say, "I have no money for lunch or gas for the week," see how they respond. Do they berate you, or do they say, "I can help you with your budget so your money will last"?

And finally, be sure your relationship is based on more than sex. In society's today we hardly ever see people who are willing to wait until they're married before sleeping together. When sex is not part of the equation, you are able to discern your real emotions. After you have sex with someone things change. The focus shifts from getting to know someone to the false intimacy. Remember, God's way is *always* the right way.

This was part of the reason Cathy had stopped dating. She was at a point of truly wanting to live a life pleasing to God. She knew that she sinned in some form - everyone does – but she wanted to draw the line at sex; for to her, that was a harder one to walk backwards. Though she loved Lewis, when they slept together prior to marriage she always felt bad and she always repented.

Abuse Is Real

Due to her past experience in law enforcement, Cathy had seen plenty of abuse – usually in the form of a bruised eye or a rape complaint. She had never known, however, that one could be beaten down with words alone. It took some time for her to realize that the way Lewis spoke to her, though he didn't curse or call her names, was in fact verbal and emotional abuse. The lessons she learned will stick with her the rest of her life; she will never, ever be abused again.

Cathy now believes the calling on her life and the type of ministry she has is being used for the Glory of God. Did it feel good? No, but she made it through by the Grace of God, and now she can use it to do His work and help others.

Abuse is when your partner lashes out with aggressive, belittling or violent behavior. This is only a power play to show you who the boss really is. After the abuse, then comes the guilt. It is so amazing what a person will do to have power.

Usually, Lewis would ask Cathy what she wanted, such as a purse or new shoes, to repair the damage his abuse had caused. That was his guilt talking, because he was afraid of being caught and facing consequences for his abusive behavior. He was never really sorry, though; it was all an act.

When people don't want to be responsible for their actions, excuses come. Excuses are what the abuser says and does to avoid taking responsibility. The abuser will even try and rationalize what they have done by using excuses and/or blame you for their behavior. This is followed by a "honeymoon period" of normal behavior.

Normal behavior is a tool used to try and keep the victim with them. They act as if nothing really happened. When it suited him, Lewis would pour on the charm so thick, just so Cathy would fall into the trap again, thinking he might change. All abusers do this to keep and regain control over the victim. You fantasize that things will be better, even "perfect." When the abuser fantasizes, it is about abusing you again. They may think about what you've done "wrong" and how they are going to make you pay. Payback could come in many ways; it depends on the abuser and their power kick.

Set-up is when the abuser sets you up and puts their plan in motion, creating a situation where they can justify abusing you. For Cathy it was like a scheme, plot or plan, and she could always feel it coming, depending on the tone of voice Lewis used. Cathy worked extremely hard at home, because she knew if there were not enough towels in the bathroom, or anything else not to his liking, a verbal putdown was forthcoming.

There are many warning signs of abuse, including a feeling of fear or anxiety about pleasing their partner; going along with everything their partner says, even if it is wrong, because they are afraid to make them upset; receiving frequent, harassing phone calls from their partner, which was a constant for Cathy. They also constantly feel the need to explain themselves in order to avoid their partner's jealousy and possessiveness; they feel restricted because their partner controls the money. Perhaps worst of all, they isolate themselves from friends and family because they are ashamed of the abuse.

Many people believe that if you are not getting hit or raped you are not being abused. That is so far from the truth. Emotionally abusive relationships can destroy your self-worth. If you feel like you have to walk around on eggshells when your mate is present, that is a sign. Cathy was often silent in their relationship because she was afraid of upsetting Lewis. Feeling belittled and controlled are other signs, and eventually lead to a life of helplessness and desperation.

People also tend to judge victims, claiming to know what they would do if they were in that situation. Unless you have walked in that person's shoes, you cannot speak on the subject. Domestic violence and abuse do not discriminate; it happens to people of all walks of life, races, religions and socioeconomic groups.

Often domestic violence escalates from threats and verbal abuse to physical violence. For example, while Lewis did not physically abuse Cathy, he did put his hands on the women after her.

Another kind abuse is when someone tries to control their partner's appearance. Lewis, for example, required Cathy to have a different hairstyle of his liking no matter how long it took. She never had to worry about gaining weight, though; because of his abusive nature she was too stressed to eat much. Since her divorce she has allowed food to become her lover and manages her eating and her weight on her own terms.

When going from being abused to being free, transformation is necessary. You have to become whole again and love you for you. It is a long and painful process, but it is worth it.

You Can Make It

Living with any form of abuse is not what and how God intended for us to live. Abuse can take a toll on your body, mind and spirit. Cathy never would have had the strength to survive all the abuse in her life, if not for her relationship from God. He is the answer, and He can give you a way of escape. Cathy knew that in all her other marriages cheating was the factor and that was a way of escape for her. Lewis, by creating a life with another person while still married, truly set her free, though in the divorce decree he flipped it and accused Cathy of being unfaithful. That truly shows what kind of man he really was.

Through God, you have the power to defeat them which is the enemy. Remember, a person can't say I love you and curse you out with the same lips. You have to take control and stop the abuse as soon as possible, not allowing the abuser to stop when their behavior benefits them.

Actions speak louder than words; how people treat you says a lot more about how they feel than what they tell you. Open the eyes God gave you and start looking at people and situations with discernment. What you see is truly what you are going to get. Once you know this, you can decide whether to accept it or not.

After being abused for a while, it can be hard to imagine that something better is out there. Take it from Cathy, there is. If you don't feel strong enough to leave for yourself, do it for your children. Abuse is often passed down from generation to generation: kids watch and hear their parent being mistreated (or mistreating someone else) and they copy that behavior.

Decide today that you are going to break that cycle of abuse before it infects your children. Unlike you, your children had no choice about where they live or who they live with. It is your responsibility to provide them with a safe, loving environment. They deserve it, and so do you.

Earlier in life Cathy had to walk away from material things to ensure a better home and life for her children. She didn't care, because she knew her number one priority was to make sure they were okay. Even in her last marriage, she could have fought Lewis for a payout of the condo or maybe even support, but she wanted something money can't buy, and that's peace.

This does not mean you have to break the cycle alone. If needed, seek help from a counselor or support group. The lack of self-worth can go back far as your childhood, and a professional can help you get to the root of your problems and eventually release them. Above all, start reading the Bible, praying and mediating on the word of God. Allow His word to penetrate your heart so your faith can grow. All you need is faith the size of a mustard seed, so if you can imagine yourself being happy, living debt-free and being safe from an abuser it can be done.

Goal-setting is important; many victims feel they cannot leave because they have nothing on their own. Remember, there is always a way out. Yes, you may have to start from scratch. Yes, it may require planning and hard work and sacrifice, but nothing is more important than your safety and your freedom. Step out in faith and believe that God will lead you through it.

Here is a powerful exercise to help get your mind and heart in the right space. Go to the mirror, look at yourself and say, "I'm free, I'm free. I'm beautiful, Jesus paid the price and I am totally free."

As long as you are on this earth you have the opportunity to be and do what you desire. It's not over until God say it's over. All your tests can be turned into a testimony to help someone else that is going through the same thing.

God can use anybody, you only have to read the word to see how many different people He used. So never feel like you are a failure because you have gotten caught up with the wrong person. We all make mistakes and hopefully we all learn from them. So if you get into one of these "We said I do but he/she didn't" situations, just know you will make it through.

Prayer for The Victim

God, thank You for blessing me another day, with life. Please forgive me for all my sins, whether committed knowingly or unknowingly.

I desire to be a better person according to Your word. I have been abused and it hurt, I need Your help to repair my heart and deliver me from that abusive spirit.

God, I know I was predestined for greatness and I have settled for less. I decree and declare that this day will be the end of the abusive cycle.

I need Your mighty power to give me the strength and the boldness I need to move forward. Please continue to protect my children and everyone that is or was affected by this abuser.

Give me divine strength to take control of this life You have given me. I surrender to You now, I cast all my cares upon You, because You care.

Thank You for opening my eyes to see what needed to be changed. Thank You for a new life and a new beginning. Nothing will go lacking because the abuser is gone. I pray my abuser gets help and is shown the light of Christ.

I believe Jesus died on the Cross for my sins, I believe He rose on that third day. I surrender, I offer my life as a living sacrifice to Him. I accept Jesus as my Lord and Savior, Amen.

Prayer for The Abuser

God, thank You for blessing me another day, with life. Please forgive me for all my sins, whether they were committed knowingly or unknowingly.

I desire to be a better person according to Your word. I have been abusing others in some form: verbal, sexual, physical or emotional. No matter what, God, they did not deserve to be treated the way I treated them.

Right now, God, I need all the help from You; I need to be led by You. Please forgive me and help the people I abused. The inward or the outward scars may still be healing on them or inside them.

God, please give them the strength to go forward. I don't want to continue hurting others. I need a heart transplant; I need to be purged. Here I am, Father, standing in the need of help. You say we have not because we ask not, so I'm asking now.

I need this cycle that I have created to end today. Lead me to the right people and the church I need to grow in. But I must surrender now; I need Your help to repair my heart and deliver me from that abuser spirit. I repent to You, God. You did not create me to be like this and I am turning around this day; no more being an abuser.

I believe Jesus died on the Cross for my sins, I believe He rose on that third day. I surrender, I offer my life as a living sacrifice to Him. I accept Jesus as my Lord and Savior, Amen.

ABOUT THE AUTHOR

Carolyn J. Galler wears many hats: Prophetess, Minister, Motivational Speaker, Christian Life Coach, Mentor, Executive Director of online Ministry and mother. She has worked in Ministry for over twenty years and has been involved in prison ministry in various states for sixteen years.

Prophetess Galler has preached in front of hundreds of people. She has been invited to be the main guest at women's conferences and events serving at-risk youth. God has blessed her with many positions, including social services aide; law enforcement officer; and the founder of U R Never Alone Outreach Ministry. She has served as a Director of Domestic Violence and Abuse Outreach Center, which provided intervention for female victims of domestic violence. She has also served as a monitor at a shelter for raped and abused women.

Ms. Galler also has personal experiences with abuse of every kind. She believes that through these trials and tribulations, God blessed her with the expertise to bring His word and healing to all people, regardless of their race, creed or religion. She loves to encourage other men and women when they are going through their storms to trust and believe these storms will pass.

Going through abuse can be shameful or embarrassing, so she tries to let people know that they are not alone. Anyone can get caught up in a situation that appears to be so great and turns out to be toxic and even dangerous. The point is to get to a place of safety and move on so we can heal.

She is a living testament to the fact that the cycle of abuse can end. There were times when she had to struggle to raise her three children, but she pressed on and knew she had to support them even if it meant working two jobs, going to their games and then cooking or providing them with supper. They were a blessing as well, for they forced her to keep moving forward, even in those times when she wanted to give up.

She wanted to show her children anything is possible if you truly believe and have a relationship with God. Many times we can put God last after we mess up, instead of asking Him what His will is before we act.

After hearing her story, many people want to know whether Ms. Galler is married now. The answer is no, not because she is bitter toward men, but because she is truly waiting on the Lord. Does the devil try to come in and present himself as someone that he isn't? Yes. But she realizes that if she focuses on God's business and put Him first, then what is meant to be, shall be. Being single doesn't mean you are messed up, it just may mean you are healthier being alone. When you are single you are better able to focus on your relationship with God, instead of focusing on a spouse. There is nothing wrong with marriage; after all, God ordained it. Make sure he/she is who God has for you, then set your standards and if he/she can't accept them, they are not the partner for you.

Currently, Ms. Galler also has a non-profit online ministry, "U R Never Alone Outreach Ministry," which was designed to allow people to be free and work through their hurts and pains, and most importantly, to know that with Jesus all things are possible.

To learn more about her work, got to:
urneveraloneoutreach.com

She can be contacted at urnaoutreach@gmail.com or via the Facebook page, U R Never Alone Outreach.

Proverbs: 18:22 NKJV
"A man who finds a wife finds a good thing and obtains favor from the Lord."

**Remember, keep the faith, believe and trust God.
You are somebody special!**

A PRAYER FROM THE AUTHOR TO YOU

Praise God for you reading and supporting the author.

She prays that you will receive an overflow of spiritual growth, love, wealth, health in your life and in the life of your family.

In the Name of Jesus, you are not at the tail, you are at the head. No matter what your situation may look like, trust God. He would not have brought you to it if He was not going to bring through it.

Just know God loves you unconditionally, and even when it seems like God is not present He is there. We thank God right now for a transformation in your life and being set free.

All strongholds are broken, and generational cures are broken and sent to the pits of hell. In Jesus' Name we ask for healing and deliverance from anything that set you apart from God.

We give God all the glory and all the praise, in Jesus' Name.
Amen.

Be Blessed
Carolyn J Galler

JOURNAL – NOTES
You Are Special

JOURNAL – NOTES
You Are Free

JOURNAL – NOTES
Let Go, Let God

_____

_____

_____

_____

_____

_____

_____

_____

_____

_____

_____

_____

_____

_____

_____

_____

_____

_____

_____

_____

_____

_____

_____

_____

_____

_____

_____

JOURNAL – NOTES
You Are Wonderful and Loved

JOURNAL - NOTES
Let The Past Stay Behind You

JOURNAL - NOTES
What's For You Is For You

JOURNAL - NOTES
Where You Live Doesn't Dictate Who You Are

_____

_____

_____

_____

_____

_____

_____

_____

_____

_____

_____

_____

_____

_____

_____

_____

_____

_____

_____

_____

_____

_____

_____

_____

_____

JOURNAL - NOTES
Live Life To The Fullest

JOURNAL - NOTES
It Only Takes Faith

JOURNAL - NOTES
If God Is For You Who Can Be Against You

JOURNAL – NOTES
You Are Wonderful

JOURNAL – NOTES
Jesus Loves You

JOURNAL – NOTES
You Will Survive

JOURNAL – NOTES
Who's Report Will You Believe

JOURNAL – NOTES
You Are Special

_____

_____

_____

_____

_____

_____

_____

_____

_____

_____

_____

_____

_____

_____

_____

_____

_____

_____

_____

_____

_____

_____

_____

_____

_____

_____

_____

_____

JOURNAL – NOTES
My Pain Don't Dictate My Future

JOURNAL – NOTES
Girl/Boy Bye, I'm Complete Without You

_____

_____

_____

_____

_____

_____

_____

_____

_____

_____

_____

_____

_____

_____

_____

_____

_____

_____

_____

_____

_____

_____

_____

_____

_____

_____

JOURNAL – NOTES
If God Said It Believe It

JOURNAL – NOTES
Thank God Daily

_____

_____

_____

_____

_____

_____

_____

_____

_____

_____

_____

_____

_____

_____

_____

_____

_____

_____

_____

_____

_____

_____

_____

_____

_____

JOURNAL – NOTES
You Are Not In That Place Anymore

JOURNAL – NOTES
I'm God's King/Queen

JOURNAL – NOTES
I Know Who I Am

JOURNAL – NOTES
Never Settle For Less

JOURNAL – NOTES
The Old Is Out And The New Is In

JOURNAL – NOTES
This Body Belongs To God

JOURNAL – NOTES
Enjoy Today Tomorrow Isn't Promised

JOURNAL – NOTES
No More Excuses

JOURNAL – NOTES
I Will Live For Christ

JOURNAL – NOTES
Peace Dwell In Me

_____
_____
_____
_____
_____
_____
_____
_____
_____
_____
_____
_____
_____
_____
_____
_____
_____
_____
_____
_____
_____
_____
_____
_____
_____
_____
_____

JOURNAL – NOTES
No More Secrets

JOURNAL – NOTES
I Am Complete In Jesus

JOURNAL – NOTES
I Have Surrendered

JOURNAL – NOTES
May God Receive All The Glory

_____
_____
_____
_____
_____
_____
_____
_____
_____
_____
_____
_____
_____
_____
_____
_____
_____
_____
_____
_____
_____
_____
_____
_____
_____
_____
_____
_____
_____

JOURNAL – NOTES
No Weapon Against Me Shall Prosper

JOURNAL – NOTES
I Do Trust God

JOURNAL – NOTES
It Was Not My Fault

JOURNAL – NOTES
It Was Only A Test

JOURNAL – NOTES
It's Time To Move On

JOURNAL – NOTES
I Forgive My Abuser

_____
_____
_____
_____
_____
_____
_____
_____
_____
_____
_____
_____
_____
_____
_____
_____
_____
_____
_____
_____
_____
_____
_____
_____
_____

JOURNAL – NOTES
I Forgive Myself

_____

_____

_____

_____

_____

_____

_____

_____

_____

_____

_____

_____

_____

_____

_____

_____

_____

_____

_____

_____

_____

_____

_____

_____

Made in the USA
Columbia, SC
27 November 2024

47320118R00086